Disadvantaged Populations And Technology In Music

VASILEIOS YFANTIS

.

ISBN-10: 1492728624
ISBN-13: 978-1492728627

DEDICATION

This book is dedicated to all the disadvantaged artists and fans that continue to enjoy the value of music through listening or recording music.

CONTENTS

ACKNOWLEDGMENTS

I would like to thank Billy James (Glass Onyon PR), Dr. Abel Usoro (University of the West of Scotland) and Dr. Dimitrios Tseles (Technological Institute of Piraeus) for their continuous support during my research. Moreover, I want to thank all the artists that agreed to get interviewed for this book.

The Change Of The Music Industry And Introduction Of New Technologies

The transition from the industrial to post industrial society affected all the light and heavy industries in a tremendous level because the changing thought patterns created a new economy based on the knowledge. Thus, all the industries were led to a new way that people, processes and products interact in the product's lifecycle.

The transformation of an industrial society to a post industrial is characterized by the fact that the new economy progressed from an economy based on manufactured products, to an economy based on virtual products, finance, services and the power of information. The most important changes that occurred during the transformation of the society are:

- Education becomes an appropriate skill to boost the new economy's progression.
- The production of ideas became as much relevant to the economic growth as the production of goods.
- Occupations that are related to the new knowledge economy like managers, scientists, IT experts become necessary for the society.

- Information and technology oriented sciences define the society's future.
- Research and development procedures are used in order to create innovative ideas.
- Human and social capitals are considered essential for the nation's economic strength.
- The infrastructure of the industrial economy was transportation, but the post industrial economy's infrastructure is communication (Bell, 1999).

The music industry as a part of the retail industry changed the music product's lifecycle according to the needs of the Information Communication Technologies. The new post industrial product lifecycle is currently based on the communication of electronic information such as MP3 or MP4 music files by using the public network of internet. Thus, the transition from the industrial society to post industrial society affected the digitization of the music in a great degree:

- The physical music products like vinyl, CDs and cassettes became digital products with the help of the electronic information that simulates the audio files. Moreover, recorded music from music studios is directly transformed into electronic information and there is no need for any additional editing before the product's distribution to the market.

- The storage needs of the music distribution are few because a computer hard disc can hold thousands of music albums instead of owning a large room to place inside all of your physical music products.
- The physical transportation of the music products became online communication with the fans who buy the electronic files.
- Fewer intermediaries exist due to the less phases of the music product's lifecycle.

The industrial lifecycle starts from the moment that music has been recorded in the music studio. Afterwards, this music is delivered in physical format to the factories so as to create a physical music format suitable for consumption (vinyl, CD, cassettes). CDs are physically distributed to the record stores and they are ready for sale. The distribution of the music products to the consumers is being implemented with the physical presence of the consumer as a requirement. Additionally, record stores can post the products through the traditional post office by charging an extra cost for this action.

Post industrial lifecycle starts again from the moment that the recording material is ready in the music studio. Of course the difference here is that there are fewer steps until the consumer finally receives the music product. The engineer in the recording studio directly converts the music into a digital format such as MP3. These music files are being sent via e-mail to the e-shops that need only the physical presence of a server to store the music files. Afterwards, web shops sell directly to the final consumer. This lifecycle is shorter than the old one and this fact minimizes the cost of the product and time needed to distribute music files to the consumers.

Communication as the infrastructure of the post industrial society and Information Technologies as the medium of communication, led to the creation of mobile computing and broadband internet connections. Internet penetration differs from country to country and it depends on various social and political factors which have an impact on the citizen's access and effective use of technology as to maximize the expected benefits for society (Xiaoming and Chow 2004).

The digital customer is more demanding now due to the fact that he is able to gather a greater amount of information which includes product availability in less time with the help of the internet. So he is able to adjust his consuming behavior through the power of information he owns now.

Broadband internet connections with fast speeds have

impacted the power of information which the customer finds available. The power of information depends on the quality and the quantity and these values increase as the speed of the transferred internet data increases. Moreover, users are now having access to streaming sound and video which affect the buying decision at a greater rate (Langer, 2002).

The other technology which has helped music industry progress is the wireless connections and the Wi-Fi networks. The wireless networks have helped the implementation of communication between customers and companies in any place around the world without any limitations. Wi-Fi has been very popular due to the introduction of mobile computing as a solution to use your computer facilities anytime and anywhere (Reza, 2005).

The three elements of mobile computing are (Bernardo and Bogliolo 2005):

- Communication: Access of a network or other communication partners without a wire because it is replaced by electromagnetic waves (Schiller, 2003).
- Devices: The variety of mobile devices that exist and have access in wireless networks.
- Applications: Applications that run partially or completely on mobile devices (Amjad, 2004).

Some of the most popular mobile devices are notebooks, tablet PCs, smart phones, personal digital assistants and other. All these devices include a small antenna in order to receive and transmit electronic data into wireless networks (Chen, 2007). They are connected with Wi-Fi or Wi-Max technologies in order to access public networks like the internet or local and wide area networks (Michael and Salter 2006). The mobile computing software that they use varies from simple spreadsheet applications to multimedia ones with which one can watch movies, play music, create blogs, and view 3D presentations and other usages.

The mobile nature of computer science has been very useful for human mobility (Kim, 2001) especially when people move from one place to the other for tourism. As the years go by and public network technologies progress at a faster rate, there is an increased quantity of information exchanged between people.

Mobile computing and networking technologies contribute equally in the globalization of the exchanged information and they also ensure an efficient way for the advantaged and disadvantaged populations to join the digital revolution. Mobile computing is enabling people to benefit from the technology in any place because today all the mobile devices are small and light so the possession of a mobile computing device has become an everyday habit. Another advantage of the technology is the fact that the greater efficiency, which Information Technology possesses today, leads computer scientists to create the different modules for customized content. This means that technology with the help of the programming languages, manages to cover different needs that the different target groups may have. The easiness of the customized content's production adjusts the technology to the local economies and so they all use a globalized technology platform.

The theory of globalization "when used in an economic context, it refers to the reduction and removal of barriers between national borders in order to facilitate the flow of goods, capital, services and labor" (ESCWA, 2011). In other words, globalization encourages the communication of the information in worldwide level and this fact allows the mobility of people, processes, products and culture around the world.

The common technology platform for all the nations that adopt the globalization model is World Wide Web and especially broadband networks. As the internet speed became faster, exchange of information and services became a reality. The broadband networks encourage commercial transactions in real time and the implementation of various types of services including entertainment. The globalized model of online entertainment boosts the economic growth of the entertainment industry and the distribution of entertainment products became digital. The digital distribution of music involves fewer intermediaries because the producer sells directly to the consumer and of course there are opportunities for the producers to break into a global market.

It is very interesting to research how the digital music model operates and how it is related to technology. The changing technology has enabled almost every new device to play music, thus the new business model in the music industry does not focus on the potentiality success of specific artists but to the music's availability. The number of available devices that play music is going to encourage the availability of music libraries that the consumers are going to access under a small monthly subscription. While, back in the 1970s and 1980s the number of music albums you owned made you an opinion leader among the social teams, the easiness of finding music today does not encourage people buying music. The consumers of today want to have access in a large variety of music and afterwards are going to decide upon buying or not a specific music track. The music labels today license their catalogue not only for downloading, but they enable access to the music for various reasons and with different price strategies.

Web 2.0 and the world of social networking empower the music library's access due to the cultural exchange that is becoming a reality through the social networking. The availability of new smart phones along with the agreements between ISPs and mobile provides contribute in the accessibility of music from technology users that own the most popular devices. So the new business model is characterized by the opportunity to access the music library from anywhere by using the internet platform and then hear the music everywhere, in any device that plays music. Internet as a platform becomes the appropriate technology tool so as to implement the model of music anywhere – music everywhere.

According to Mark Piibe, who has served head of digital business development in EMI Music: "The record industry is more open to new models now than it has ever been. We are experimenting in ways that we wouldn't have considered three years ago, and we are also getting a lot more sophisticated about the differences between markets" (Moore, 2011). The issue of access to music has been in the news stories for a long time, but the old business model allowed access to music catalogs only by specific devices. The popularity of new gadgets and the availability of many different music devices, led the music industry to change the model and enable access to the music libraries from all the available devices. It is interesting to realize that the consumers have changed their consumption habits and they prefer different ways of how and where to listen to music. According to Francis Keeling, who has served vice president of Universal Music Group International: "The most successful network operators will be those who can offer connected devices to the living room and the portable device. We have seen rapid developments on mobile platforms, and key to the development of music services for the future will be the TV set top box" (Moore, 2011). The new environment for the music consumption is mainly based on the internet that is the most popular network medium at the moment, which implements the digital music model of accessing music from anywhere.

Disadvantaged Populations And Technology Access

The term disadvantaged populations describes the groups of people that have denied access to the tools needed for self sufficiency (Mayer, 2003). The topics that are associated with self sufficiency are: Autonomy, incentive, responsibility, self respect, health, education, information, employment, capital and much more (Mayer, 2003). Self sufficiency describes the state that the human survival depends only on personal soft or hard skills and not on external factors such as support or other kind of help. The prevention from the self sufficiency goal is usually caused by the lack of availability or low access to specific resources (Mayer, 2003). The resources needed for the disadvantaged population in order to adopt self sufficiency are (Mayer, 2003):

1. Autonomy or Non-dependence: The term of autonomy is described as the opportunity of a social group to act according to their will and be free to express themselves through their activities.

2. Incentive for development: This means that the social groups have to keep on believing that their dreams will come true and their mission will be fulfilled. They actually require a trigger which will

boost their efforts and cause them to try harder for personal development.

3. Decision-making responsibility: The groups should contribute within the democratic processes that leads to decision making, as this will help them to feel empowered from feeling empowered, giving them a sense of responsibility for their own lives.

4. Self-respect: People need to respect their own entity as if they respect themselves, they are able to respect society and offer their knowledge towards the progress of society. Lack of self respect can prevent them from being powerful enough to offer their effort in life.

5. Community of support: The term of community unites people under the umbrella of support and all the social groups benefit from the meaning of caring for one another. The social groups have more chances to survive by creating communities and supporting each other, than being isolated and struggling to live in the modern world.

6. Health: The quality of health viewed as a basic factor for safe and fast access to self sufficiency because illness can be a barrier which may hold people back from having a normal life. Disabled persons face many difficulties for self sufficiency, especially in societies where disability is considered taboo and people tend to criticize ill persons that

receive medical treatment.

7. Education: The value of learning the society's culture has a positive influence on people who want to reach a level of self sufficiency. Educated persons are capable of critically reviewing the ideas and ethics, thus they become more tolerant towards the society and fight for what they believe in.

8. Information: Awareness of information is synonymous with the power of knowledge, as well informed people tend to adopt the know how of success and they are able to maintain a better quality of daily life.

9. Employment: When someone is in employment, then that person often feels a sense of security and is better equipped to plan for the future. When the job is promising and career oriented, additional advantages exist, such as freedom of choice, spiritual satisfaction, joy and much more.

10. Capital: Financial security tends to protect people from poverty and offers them more opportunities for a happier life than just to satisfy the basic needs of survival. Capital is the means to reach the level of hoping for the next goal unless an emotional or health barrier prevents you from that.

11. Responsive support systems: These are the systems which can support societies and give them

access to resources of food, water, clothing, transportation and cultural activities.

The advantages of these resources, prevent someone from being disadvantaged but in order to implement the adoption of these resources, social groups have to adjust each resource according to their culture. The diversity of cultures among the different social groups may act as barrier for self sufficiency as each group has different beliefs and thought patterns according to factors such as sex and race.

Despite the great importance of technology in the music industry, the availability, access and use of technology in a worldwide level differs from country to country. The whole phenomenon has been termed as the digital divide by experts and according to NTIA (2002) is defined as: "The disparity of use of the internet and unequal access to information communications technology".

The more developed countries are in a state of possessing and using technology on a larger scale than emerging countries, so the "big brother" is responsible to help the small brother in order to have a happy and balanced family. There are various factors that affect the digital divide between countries, but the most important are income and education:

Income (Norris, 2001): e.g. The monthly salary of an individual or a family not being enough for the main needs as to have money left over to purchase a computer.

According to the psychologist Abraham Maslow and his theoretical model, people hierarchy their needs and they satisfy the basic needs such as food and water and then proceed to the other needs. Maslow's model is depicted in the shape of a pyramid where the basic physiological needs are at the bottom and as we move higher in the hierarchy there are other needs that deal with safety, belonging, esteem and self actualization. If someone needs internet in order to gain an income, then maybe internet could be placed in the Maslow's pyramid as well. This person uses the technology as a medium to gain income and satisfy the basic needs of the pyramid, food and water. Otherwise, people that their work is not related to technology they do not need internet so desperately because income, which contributes in the satisfaction of the basic needs, does not include technology as a helpful tool.

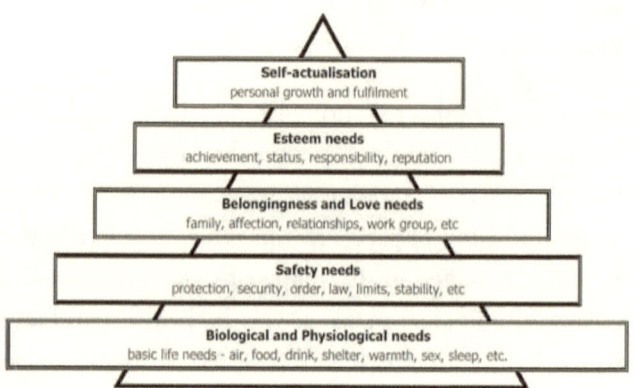

Figure: Abraham Maslow's pyramid of needs

(Source: Rakowski, N. (2011) Maslow's Hierarchy of Needs Model - the Difference of the Chinese and the Western Pyramid on the Example of Purchasing Luxurious Products, p.4)

The economic difference between low income and high income households in USA is a factor that contributes in the digital divide and it has to be taken into account very seriously. Online activities and high tech gadgets are occupied mainly by people who have the income to spend and have already covered their physiological needs.

Education (Jones and Sallis, 2002): e.g. Countries based on agricultural production do not believe that the technological education provides skills for future human resources.

The use of technology in education is a factor that affects the technology's usage in the other stages of life as well. There are theories which insist that the placement of computers in classes during the educational process, improve the familiarity between the students / teachers and technology (Monroe, 2004) but this fact is not enough to close the digital divide. The term of digital divide does not cover only the access to technology but the effective usage of technology too. This means that is not enough to offer only free internet access to the students so as to browse and play games with their friends, but to educate them in learning to use the technology effectively (Quinones and Kirshshtein 1998). The effective use of technology includes the adoption of special skills in order to detect if the electronic information that was found, is accurate and appropriate with the search question (Besser, 2011). There is an interesting research that shows the contribution of education regarding the appropriateness of the web content. The Children's Partnership conducted a research that lasted 6 months and included both primary and secondary research. The primary research was implemented by interviewing low income internet users and technology leaders while the secondary research included references to previously published research and independent analysis of more than 1000 websites (Children's Partnership, 2011). The findings of the research that was published on March 2000 (Lazarus

& Mora, 2000) reveal the following barriers (Besser, 2011):

- Lack of local information: The content of the web information is not always local oriented but there is a globalized philosophy about communication, job finding and much more. Thus, people that are not educated enough in order to accept that internet is a global and not a local phenomenon, hesitate to accept internet technology as a tool for their daily information and tend to trust only, the local word of mouth sources.

- Lack of local information based on basic literacy level: The main online content has been written for people that have basic or above literacy skills. So people that didn't have the opportunity to attend a school or stopped the education process for other reasons are almost unable to understand the published information on the websites.

- Limited information for non English speaking internet users: Due to the global type of information that is published online, most of the web publishers choose to use the English language. Today there are about 32 million people in USA that English is not their first language and they are not able to read the web's content and benefit from the useful info. The lack of English language learning prevents them from wanting to join the internet revolution.

- Lack of information that was created in a culturally appropriate way: There is a small quantity of online content about ethnically diverse American communities created by the same communities.

Other factors that contribute in the digital divide are:

Geographic location (Dutton, 2005): For example, countries that are located away from hi tech countries remain backwards in terms of technology updates.

Cultural (Iskander, Kapila and Karim, 2010): For example, local religious beliefs treat technology as something against their religion.

Political (Chadwick, 2009): For example, military governments are afraid to offer to the citizen's access to new information through the internet so as to prevent them from expressing anti-governmental ideas.

It is very important to realize that a disadvantaged population is currently affected by the digital divide and this is a barrier for the progress of both music commerce and technology. The more people deny the introduction of new technologies, the more these persons are going to face various issues in the near future. The population of disabled people worldwide was estimated to be 650 million in 2009 (Council of Europe, 2009) and indeed they have the same rights for access to entertainment services.

The large number of disabled members of the society and their special needs translates to immense spending, which also fulfills their entertainment and pleasure needs. According to the results of the 11th Caribbean Conference on Sustainable Tourism Development only in UK there were 2.7 million disabled people in 2010 who travel annually and in the US there were more than 22 million people with the same consuming behavior (Caribbean 360, 2010). The Canadians with disabilities are spending $25 billion annually as consumers and they also travel along with friends or relatives. This is an important factor because apart from the predicted income of the disabled persons who travel, an additional income is going to exist from the persons that accompany the disabled community. The most important problems that disabled people encounter when they travel are classified into 3 categories:

- Social Acceptance (Tregaskis, 2004): Countries with low vertical social mobility where their citizens do not have the opportunity to move up to the social hierarchy and who look down on disabled people and treat them with hostility and negative empathy because they believe that these people cannot improve their quality of life.

- Special Needs (Langan, 1998): Disabled people may need special requirements such as wheelchairs in order to ease their transportation needs. Also the streets or the pavements have to be user–friendly in terms of construction. Moreover, other facilities such as elevators in high buildings have to exist.

- Lack of Information (Turmusani, 2003): This is a much underrated issue, but surely it may be one of the reasons that prevent them from traveling. The disabilities they have may cause them insecurity about what kind of risks they may encounter or face when traveling abroad.

Web communities are very popular among the disabled because they tend to be more democratic than other types of communication (Delanty, 2010). However, there is a high percentage of responsibility when they write their points of view about various kinds of issues. There is a strong community feeling because if they help each other, all the members of the community can benefit from the process. This in turn builds social trust with the help of technology and it improves the community's point of view towards e-democracy and digital society.

Mobile technology through smart phones or tablets is

known as the "Robin Hood" that will steal all the wealth of information from the rich and offer it to the poor. There are various examples of mobile technology's usage for disabled people while they are traveling.

iPad is a tablet computer that was created by Apple and initially used for reading e-books, listening to music and browsing the Web (Jesperson, 2010). It is very small and light weight (around 700 grams) and operates via a multi touch screen. It also has a wireless connection and a few of the models have 3G access included as well. Regardless of the fact that many people consider it a high tech gadget, according to the director of Trace Research and the Development Center at the University of Wisconsin in Madison: "iPad can solve the communication problems of many disabled people" (Jesperson, 2010). She bases her point of view on the nature of people that have communication problems, who work better with the external human environment through touch screens. Such people include those with dyslexia, autism, or a paralyzing condition who, for example, may use the screen to speak for them by writing text or creating graphics instead of expressing their ideas verbally.

This is considered to be extremely important for use in traveling as there can be various moments when the disabled person has an emergency incident and wants to communicate this with the tour operator. In this situation, mobile technology has a serious role in crisis management by communicating the issues in an effective way so that the project manager (tour operator) is able to address the problem.

iPhone is another smart phone designed by Apple and maybe the most well known on the market of gadgets, as it operates more than just a phone, it includes a camera, Wi-Fi availability, media player for music and video and much more. So it is like an all in one device for entertainment. The success of the iPhone is based on the famous applications that are made for this device. Among these applications, dynamic controls is a really helpful application for disabled people in wheelchairs who are going to travel (Dynamic Europe, 2010). It is an application that you install on the iPhone via Bluetooth and you can view in real time the status, which include the speed and direction, of the wheelchair. Other features of the application include a compass heading, a seat adjustment indicator and a one touch emergency contact. This is a very useful application while travelling with the tour group as it prevents the user from facing unexpected problems on the road. It can also offer entertainment for the disabled person if he considers it as a stimulation of car racing devices where the high tech drivers have complex devices in the car to ensure the best performance of the engine.

The more the market of mobile apps (applications) continues to grow, the more are different types of applications going to be made for disabled people. The simplicity of installation along with the familiar interface of most mobile devices makes them user friendly for disabled people. The contribution of mobile technology designed for disabled people is making E-Entertainment more accessible for these people and no doubt they should enjoy more facilities during their trip.

Context awareness is another efficient way of meeting the information needs of disabled people. Context awareness technology facilitates information acquisition and execution by supporting interoperability between users and devices based on the user's context (Lee, Ho Kang and Slezak, 2010). This is used mainly in mobile devices and detects where you are located, who is beside you and what kind of useful resources are around you. The intelligence of the context aware system enables it to pick up how many people are around, the level of noise, the social environment, the weather and other information that can lead to wise decision making. The context awareness is implemented through special software that is installed in the mobile device and records the user's behaviour and stores a file on her phone without distributing this information in any public network except there is a conscious goal to transfer the information over a network to a central server, for instance.

This software is very useful when someone (disabled or not) is travelling in foreign countries where he/she does not know the place and it is not easy to navigate around and find interesting places. For instance, if someone is walking in West Hollywood and looking for an entertainment venue, then his phone with the help of GPS detects the area, gains access to a local cultural database and a notification pops up that offers directions to an exciting bar in Sunset Strip. Of course, the user can always have access to the stored info and change it according to his new preferences.

The basic elements that are needed by the context aware system are low cost, low battery and a few sensors like GPS, accelometers, cameras and other features. These sensors collect various types of data and store it in a safe place for a specific period (Wood, 2008). The system combines the data and waits to see if the person is going to change his behavior regarding the use of the mobile device (Wood, 2008).

The accelometer is able to detect whether the person is walking, sitting or running (Li, 2009). There are also physiological measures which detect someone's temperature and heart rate so that the system can ascertain if the person is relaxed or stressed. The audio measurements from the sensors are able to inform the system if the user is chatting or listening to music, the video sensor informs the system through the camera if the person is alone in a room or with others. All this data is mixed with the user's behavior and transformed into information. This is useful data for the system to make decisions and recommend various proposals to the user through notifications on the screen.

The Intel company has developed two very useful context awareness projects that help travelers, which include the following (Stone in Science, 2010):

The Personal Vacation Assistant is a device that is documenting the experience of travelling. It uses a combination of data through the sensors of GPS and the camera along with a combination of data with calendar and food preferences. During travel, the system can make suggestions to the user on where to go and eat or have a drink. The impressive feature is that after the trip is over, the PVA will create a blog full of videos and photos.

SENS is a mobile device that has been created in order for users to share information with his friends. The innovation is the use of animated avatars that represent the user and what he is doing. Thus, when the user is running, for example, the SENS displays a running avatar on the screen.

The context awareness system becomes beneficial for all disabled people that use mobile devices when they travel because it fills the gap of missing information. The use of mobile devices or software to gain access to this information enhances mobile computing, which contributes to E-Tourism as a helpful tool.

Mobile computing is the element of computer science which can improve a disabled person's life by helping them to become more independent and able to go out and enjoy life more, being more socially active. They have the same rights for entertainment as anybody else does. The mobile devices and the special mobile software are designed based on their need for social or human movement and so improve their quality of life.

Overcoming The Technology Access To Music?

The digital divide is an issue that affects the sector of e-commerce because the non effective use or the lack of technology prevents the disadvantaged population from accessing music. Nowadays, music is being produced, distributed and consumed through the use of technology. Even the traditional music activities such as the live shows are affected by the new technologies: The web-casting through the internet gives the opportunity to attend the concert that is happening somewhere on earth!

John Fisher developed a theoretical model about how people deal with the personal change and first presented this theory at the Personal Construct Congress in Berlin (1999), this model is based on the theory of the Personal Construct Psychology (Business balls, 2011). According to the Personal Construct Psychology in order to understand and communicate with people we have to understand how they view their world and what kind of meaning do they attach to their environment (Business balls, 2011). Every person has a subjective way that views the world which it is a result of previous personal experiences and defines the way that the same person is going to deal with the world in the future. The main difference between the classic psychology and the personal construct psychology is that while the classic theory focus on our past experiences so as to predict the future, construct psychology considers the personal beliefs as not static values due to the constantly changing environment. So the personal behavior is a sum of actions that have the roots in the past experience and the current situation, thus the person in not trapped due to his past experiences. According to John Fisher, there is a climate of emotional stages that the person has to deal with while he faces a personal change (Business balls, 2011):

1. Anxiety and denial: When people do not have sufficient information about the personal change they become anxious and deny the existence of a change by continuing the use of old habits and practices.

2. Happiness: During this stage, people feel happy because their point of view about the disadvantages of the old model was loud enough so as to persuade the insiders to change the current situation.

3. Fear: The potential change is going to affect the way that people are going to act after the implementation of the new tactic and practices. The new personal behavior is possibly going to change the way that the external environment of friends and colleagues view these persons, thus the

question about "the day after" makes them afraid of the future.

4. Threat: The new environment after the change is going to affect people's life and the old habits are going to be buried in the past. The threat here is if the new environment is better than the old one.

5. Guilt and disillusionment: The changing environment makes people conduct an objective self review and decide if the new environment is close to their set of personal goals or if it alienates them from their personal beliefs. The guilt is very characteristic in the idea that with the adoption of the new system, may keep away from what they want to succeed in life. If their personal beliefs do not meet the philosophy of the new system, then disillusionment comes up and people are disappointed with themselves.

6. Depression and hostility: The guilt and disillusionment during the comparison between the meeting of the personal beliefs with the old system and the disagreement of the same beliefs with the new system causes an internal war to the affected persons. The dilemma between holding back and carrying on with the uncertainty of the new system makes them sad and depressed. The continued effort to adjust to a new system

that is unable to satisfy the personal goals leads people to the use of the old practices by underrating the new system and being hostile towards the new practices.

7. Gradual Acceptance: Persons start to realize that the change is occurring and now they position themselves in the future, according to the philosophy of the new system.

8. Moving Forward: People realize that the change has a lot to offer for their future due to the featured advantages and they want to be part of the change by contributing in the transformation from the old system to the new one.

John Fisher's theory model makes a point of showing that each change whether if it is small or big, it affects people in a different level and progressively they adopt the change by moving forward and getting involved in the implementation of the change. Of course, there is always the risk of getting stuck in a specific stage and not adopt the philosophy of the new system. That is why it is important to detect the stage that each person or social team belongs to and then define a strategy to solve the issue and make them continue to the next stage until they reach the last stage of moving forward.

Disadvantaged populations are considered the next big thing for the music industry due to the potential size of the music market, but the digital divide is a barrier which prevents them from joining the new digital music evolution. The lack of technology access by the disadvantaged populations is usually caused by external factors that are mentioned in the analysis of the digital divide. However, the non efficient use of technology is an issue that needs further exploration. The way that people view technology and the change that is going to affect their current status of life, changes their current use of the technology as well. If the technology is a value that meets their personal beliefs and satisfies the ideal goals, then the involved persons are going to adopt technology and use it efficiently by concentrating how can benefit from the technology's advantages. On the other hand, if technology is considered as a negative value for their life, then these persons are going to insist on the non efficient use of technology. Technology adoption is a crucial factor that is going to affect the new model of the music industry, which offers access to music from anywhere and in any device. If the disadvantaged populations do not escape from "the non efficient use of technology" part of the digital divide, then the new business model of the music industry is going to fail. John Fisher's model is going to focus on the disadvantaged population's point of view about the change in the technology and how do they feel about it.

The adaptation of John Fisher's model in the current

effort leads us to make 8 hypotheses based on the 8 emotional states that exist when a person is dealing with a personal change. In our hypotheses, when disadvantaged populations deal with the change of the music industry's technology, they may find themselves in one of the 8 emotional stages. Thus the question here is:

1. How the populations that suffer from the digital divide, adapt to the change in the music industry?

And of course the 8 hypotheses are:

H1: The disadvantaged population feels anxiety and denial.

H2: The disadvantaged population feels happiness.

H3: The disadvantaged population feels fear.

H4: The disadvantaged population feels threat

H5: The disadvantaged population feels guilt and disillusionment.

H6: The disadvantaged population feels depression and hostility.

H7: The disadvantaged population feels gradual acceptance.

H8: The disadvantaged population feels moving forward.

The answer to one of those hypotheses requires a scientific methodology and a number of disadvantaged persons as a sample population. This is a long term plan which is doable from a scientific perspective, but requires to take into account permissions from persons or organizations. I decided to leave the scientific part of my question for later use and asked help about the issue from several musicians. My scope is to understand how musicians consider their relationship with the technology and if they have any concerns of the disadvantaged fans and their access to music. The results of the interviews may not define precisely the emotional state of the disadvantaged populations regarding the music access. However, the empirical data of the interviews will reveal new sides of the problem for further research. I sent questionnaire invitations to hundreds of popular artists about this research. The rule was simple: Everyone had to answer the same 7 questions about technology. Some of the artists feared of being inappropriate persons for the questions. Some others, just declined for personal or non personal reasons. The brave musicians that answered my questions are presented in the following section of the book. I want to thank all of them for participating in my research and helping raise the importance of the issue due to ethical, artistic and scientific reasons. The musicians received the same 7 questions so as to make sure that everybody is treated in the same way, regardless of his commercial value as an artist.

Interview Questions

1. How would you describe the term technology?

2. How do you react when dealing with a new technology?

3. How would you consider the right use of technology?

4. How technology affects the music industry?

5. What would be the effects of the imbalance in the access and right use of technology in the music industry?

6. What are the main reasons for people that avoid the modern technology in the music industry?

7. How do you think that disadvantaged persons could use technology for accessing the music?

The Interviews

ACID MOTHERS TEMPLE

1. How would you describe the term technology?

No idea

2. How do you react when dealing with a new technology?

I'm really anachronism, so I don't want to have dealing with any new technology…

3. How would you consider the right use of technology?

Just "not too much!"

4. How technology affects the music industry?

No idea… cos many people prefer the records (vinyls) and cassette tapes again! Also me too, I haven't bought any CD disc for a long time, and I have never downloaded any music by digital distributers. I buy only vinyls.

5. What would be the effects of the imbalance in the access and right use of technology in the music industry?

No idea. I prefer just "hand up" with "face to face".

6. What are the main reasons for people that avoid the modern technology in the music industry?

Cos too much…! Music and music business should be just simple originally.

7. How do you think that disadvantaged persons could use technology for accessing the music?

If they want, they can do it. It means not just about it… If people want absolutely, they can do anything!

CHAOSTAR

1. How would you describe the term technology?

Technology is the science that exploits the power of electricity. Whenever we refer to technology we talk about all those evolutions and improvements that took place after the extensive use of electricity in any kind of industry. Music industry, of course, is not an exception.

2. How do you react when dealing with a new technology?

I always try to find all the hidden potentials of new technology. I believe that there is a reason for an improvement or a renovation in any kind of electronic procedure. It is hard in the beginning to adapt myself, but then I always find a way to use it.

3. How would you consider the right use of

technology?

There is not a right use of technology. There is right use on everything in our lives. All the industries must make a thoughtful and careful use of everything according to all the legitimate restrictions. Apart from that there is also the ethical part that plays an important role. Whatever we do in this world must have to be done in a way that doesn't harm the environment or disrespect other people. That is a general rule, at least to me and that is the one I would suggest for all uses.

4. How technology affects the music industry?

The same way it affects the world the last 100 years, when the electricity goes deeply and daily into our lives. Radically. Technology gives music a different "colour" and differentiate it a lot form the analog instruments and the traditional musical results. The basic point is that technology liberates the expressions and the imagination to roll into the music. Sounds that you would have never imagined can be created through the "furnace" of technology. The composer now has in the hands a variety of sounds that gives the ability to create multiple and different result. Moreover, technology inherited humanity with extreme music programs for the PCs that can make life easier. Imagine that every composer who wants to use an orchestra, can do it easily by using the libraries that those PC programs have at our disposal. Isn't that amazing? An "access to all" kind of music? That wouldn't have happened without the invasion of electricity in music. Of course, there are multiple drawbacks concerning that, but this is another story.

5. What would be the effects of the imbalance in the access and right use of technology in the music industry?

Exactly what I was talking about before. It is nice that the access into "sounds" is easier, but in the near future we would have at least 6.000.000 musicians out there. I don't know if that is bad, but definitely it will set new standards in finding a good music. When in future everyone will be able to create music, then how are the extremely talented and distinguished guys going to stand out? That theme arises many questions and I certainly cannot answer it easily.

6. What are the main reasons for people that avoid the modern technology in the music industry?

Probably cause they can't stand the new way of thinking regarding music. But sooner or later they will not have any other choice. They would have definitely to follow the new era of music with technology.

7. How do you think that disadvantaged persons could use technology for accessing the music?

???

DAVE KILMINSTER

1. How would you describe the term technology?

A means to an end... a convenience...

2. How do you react when dealing with a new technology?

I'm always a little wary I guess... for example, in my particular field new technology has produced transistor amps, modeling amps, digital amps... constantly striving and searching for something better... but undoubtedly the best sounding amps (in my opinion) are the ones based on the old designs from the sixties!!! Those little antiquated valves they used to produce something that all the new technology in the world has yet to equal...

3. How would you consider the right use of technology?

For me technology should be something that enhances the creative process... something that gives wings to your imagination...

4. How technology affects the music industry?

Well, I guess it makes a show like 'The Wall - Live' possible... which is an incredible achievement by Roger. He masterminded this wonderful concept, and technology made it all possible.

Unfortunately, technology also makes it possible for talentless idiots become pop stars, as there's no need to be able to sing in tune any more... 'autotune' has changed a lot of things.

5. What would be the effects of the imbalance in the access and right use of technology in the music industry?

Just switch on the Radio and listen to the music that's in the charts... they ALL have this horrible autotune effect on the vocals... it's obviously not the fault of technology, but it's taken all the soul, personality, passion and spirit out of any vocal performance. You might as well be listening to an automated telephone answer machine!! That feels very imbalanced to me... but I guess it's like photos in magazines now... it's very rare to find a picture that hasn't been heavily photoshopped and airbrushed!!!

For me personally the 'right' use of technology is something like composing a piece for an orchestra, and then (as I couldn't really afford to hire a hundred top class musicians for an afternoon) being able to produce those sounds I'm hearing on a keyboard... that's a wonderful thing.

6. What are the main reasons for people that avoid the modern technology in the music industry?

There are lots of reasons... I think technology scares a lot of people!! Some people think that by using technology they'll somehow lose their soul in the process.... That the emotional content will be lost... maybe for older musicians/artists, it gets more difficult to change and adapt as you get older? Or sometimes (like in the case of guitar amplifiers) it's just because the designers got it right the first time, and there's no real need to look any further...

Another example would be the electric guitar... despite all the new inventions, designs and breakthroughs concerning the electric guitar, the instruments that are still the most popular are very similar to the original versions produced back in the fifties!!!

7. How do you think that disadvantaged persons could use technology for accessing the music?

Have you seen the film Jason Becker: Not Dead Yet? It's an incredible, inspiring true story about this incredibly gifted guitarist that is struck down at the height of his career with amyotrophic lateral sclerosis, leaving him totally paralysed. He was given three to five years to live (that was in 1991) but he's still alive, and still composing!! He and his Father developed a system of communication via his eyes (the only part of his body, he can move), and through that communication and the use of computers Jason can still create music... I can't think of a better example of technology helping to access and create music.

ERIC NORLANDER

1. How would you describe the term technology?

I think of the word as a synonym for "tool." A simple lever is technology, so is an iPhone.

2. How do you react when dealing with a new technology?

I often react with a familiar combination of excitement and fear. I am excited about the possibilities a new technology will bring, but I fear what effect it will have on my status quo. MP3 recordings were that way. It was exciting that you could transmit and store music in such a small file size, but it was scary that this file format would change the music industry as we knew it, and likely not for the better.

3. How would you consider the right use of

technology?

Technology is a form of power, and power must be used responsibly. Technology is of course amoral, so it is up to the user to wield it for good or evil. That can even be deconstructed into the idea of using something for the greater good or for selfish personal gains.

4. How technology affects the music industry?

Inevitably, when you make something easier, the quality decreases. In 1950, if you wanted to record a piece of music, you had to perform it live with its complete arrangement from top to bottom. That made musicians work very hard -- often for their whole lives -- to become masters at their craft. Now with everything from Autotune to loop libraries, it becomes much easier to create something that sounds good. You don't have to work nearly as hard for it, and somehow that results in music with less soul, less inspiration, less commitment overall. One would have to ask the question of the body of work Mozart would have created with a modern DAW. Would it have been as good in the end? Maybe, but maybe not!

5. What would be the effects of the imbalance in the access and right use of technology in the music industry?

That is an easy question to answer. When technology

becomes a substitute for talent and inspiration, then that technology is wrongly used. It's not the technology itself that is good or bad; Technology is amoral as I said above. It's how it is used that matters.

6. What are the main reasons for people that avoid the modern technology in the music industry?

I think artists like to stick with what they know. Just because they don't use the latest and greatest technology does not mean they are luddites. For a lot of artists, getting the sound they want is critical. If that means using a guitar from the 1950s and an amp from the 1970s, then that is the best way for that artist. And if another artist can get the same inspiration from plugging a modern guitar into their computer, that is also good. There is a great old expression that is particularly relevant here, "It ain't the fiddle, it's the fiddler."

7. How do you think that disadvantaged persons could use technology for accessing the music?

Music creation is all about inspiration and talent. If a poor person or a disabled person has access to cheaper or more readily-available tools, then their talent and inspiration can be realized where in the past it may not have. That is a wonderful benefit of technology.

www.eriknorlander.com
www.facebook.com/erik.norlander.artist.page

GREG KIHN

1. How would you describe the term technology?

Merriam Webster Dictionary defines Technology as (1) the practical application of knowledge in a particular area: engineering (2) A manner of accomplishing a task using technical processes. I would widen that definition by adding that, from my experience, technology is a means to an end. My career has spanned several generations of technology. Remember, I started off making analogue recordings on 2-inch multi-track magnetic tape on old 16 track Ampex tape machines. So, in my case, the method that I use to record may be completely different, but my job - writing songs and making music - is unchanged. Only the method has changed.

2. How do you react when dealing with a new technology?

I am resistant to new technology and I don't know why. Seems like every new breakthrough encroaches more and more on my personal freedom. Privacy has become an issue. I maintain a passel of social media site, but it is maintained by a hired webmaster/marketing guy who actually does the heavy lifting. All I do is create content - write daily blogs, etc. By the way - there's that word again - Content. It's all about content. Whether its songs, novels, blog postings, short stories, whatever, you are judged by the quality of your content. If you have nothing to say, all the technology in the world can't help you.

3. How would you consider the right use of technology?

The forward movement of technology has become accelerated. Now, it changes constantly. I'd say the best use is to facilitate your message. For instance, I have a novel that came out on September 3, 2013 called RUBBER SOUL, which is a Beatles novel - a work of fiction with the Beatles as characters in the story. I am using every available venue to get the message out to PREORDER THE BOOK ON AMAZON: http://www.amazon.com/Rubber-Soul-Greg-Kihn/dp/1624670946/ref=sr_1_1?s=books&ie=UTF8&qid=1370035844&sr=1-1&keywords=greg+kihn+rubber+soul. Since all the presales are credited to the first day of release, it will boost the book up the Amazon charts where it will gather momentum. So, I'm doing internet interviews, radio interviews, podcasts, YouTube video announcements and readings from the books and playing old interviews with surviving members of the Beatles that lead to the inspiration for the book itself, social media, blogging, TV interviews, everything under the sun to get the message out. The right use of technology is whatever you use it for to promote your project. Content is king.

4.   How technology affects the music industry?

It has turned it on its ear. It is now possible to record an album (even the word "album" is archaic since we now deal in digital sound files) on a laptop computer with just a couple of decent microphones. Digital recording and editing have made it so much easier to record. They even have pitch correction (auto-tune) for voices so you don't even have to sing on key anymore. On the other hand, downloading songs for free on the Internet robs singers and songwriters of revenue. There's a whole generation of kids today that believe in their heart-of-hearts that all music should be free. Tell that to the Rolling Stones.

5.   What would be the effects of the imbalance in the access and right use of technology in the music industry?

In a perfect world, new bands who want to gain an audience would put music up for free on the Internet, while established bands like The Greg Kihn Band (who are no longer looking for exposure) will charge.

6.   What are the main reasons for people that avoid the modern technology in the music industry?

Fear. The old time record labels, see it as a threat. New bands see it as a boon. I don't think they understand it yet. Plus technology is moving so fast now that it is hard to keep up.

7. How do you think that disadvantaged persons could use technology for accessing the music?

Disadvantaged people get the full benefit of the new technology. It is now possible to do anything that requires a computer at home, so they wouldn't have to leave the house. For instance, I do a podcast out of my house, I have an ISDN line so I can do live radio anywhere in the world, I write my books here, I record musical demos on my computer, I create content, and communicate with the rest of the world from here, the comfort of my own home.

HARALD GROSSKOPF

1. How would you describe the term technology?

Technology is a tool that humans permanently developed since their earliest existence to ease any kind of physical strength that is necessary to reach an aim.

2. How do you react when dealing with new technology?

Curious, distrustful, timid and expectant.

3. How would you consider the right use of technology?

OK, when expanding or emotional, cultural and consciousness horizon. Not OK, when effectively killing neighbors.

4. How technology affects the music industry?

Not really sure about this. The invention of the turntable created the music superstar and in consequence probably killed the live event. Newest technology socialized the production tools. Everybody can record with few investments!

The unlimited accessibility to music in these days is just about killing its valency. You don`t have to save money to buy a record. You don`t even have to leave the house. Even being out of the house this accessibility isn`t limited...... In my hypothesis the invention of storable music will kill the music industry in its current form sooner or later, if not already done.

5. What would be the effects of the imbalance in the access and right use of technology in the music industry?

As I already mentioned, it will damage musics valency and as a consequence, also will cause loss on emotional intensity, music use to exercise on us.

6. What are the main reasons for people that avoid the modern technology in the music industry?

Demonisation, born out of inexperience. Conservative adherence to the elderly, like: The day before yesterday everything was better - attitude.

7. How do You think that disadvantaged persons could use technology for accessing the music?

I am disadvantaged, regarding the fact, that I never learned an instrument in a music school, or on universities. Although I do not feel discriminated at all, I rather feel favored, because I am not limited by traditional music structures, You usually learn with institutionalized music training. So I address to the handicapped, get a computer and create music, even if You are just able to do it with one finger, or with the help of a stick between Your lips. Music is joy. In the end, it´s about to vibrate air molecules to transport emotion. No matter, weather You do it with the help of computers through a loudspeaker, or the soundboard of a violin.

KANE ROBERTS

1. How would you describe the term technology?

A rehash of ancient tools that increase our ability to create art. (Without supermarkets the cellist would have to hunt for food which would greatly cut into her/his practice time.)

2. How do you react when dealing with a new technology?

My nature pushes me towards hopeful expectations, appreciation for legitimate progress and a tendency to imagine version 2.0.

3. How would you consider the right use of technology?

The application of newer technologies should be wide open or at least free of agenda driven (restrictive) judgments.

4. How technology affects the music industry?

It enables new ways to re-create that which already exists in nature.

5. What would be the effects of the imbalance in the access and right use of technology in the music industry?

Limitations are the harsh producers of any creative industry. It demands that the 100 million dollar hit film stand face to face with the 17 thousand dollar hit film.

6. What are the main reasons for people that avoid the modern technology in the music industry?

Comfort zones.

7. How do you think that disadvantaged persons could use technology for accessing the music?

Technology is a broad definition of whatever tools we have at our beck and call. An acoustic guitar or viola are examples of technological advancements. A truly creative person with limited access is far more advantaged than the less creative individual with excessive cutting edge equipment

MIKE HOWLETT

1. How would you describe the term technology?

Technology, in reference to music and musical practice, covers areas such as recording technologies

– analog and digital signals and their processing, digital audio workstations, audio processing and management software like ProTools, Logic etc – distribution technologies including formats - .aif, .wav, .mp3 etc – and of course, online delivery formats and software such as iTunes, Spotify, YouTube etc

2. How do you react when dealing with a new technology?

I use these technologies on a daily basis and regard them as tools of my art and craft.

3. How would you consider the right use of technology?

The right use of technology is any use that is applied to the realization of a creative idea in a communicable form.

4. How technology affects the music industry?

Currently, digital technology has caused a massive collapse in revenue streams for the music industry because music files can be easily transferred with no loss of quality from the first digital form and have been hard to restrict. However, gradually new systems are developing that are generating new revenue streams, such as YouTube paying a proportion of advertising revenue to content providers, iTunes, which has taken over the role of distributor from the traditional record companies, and online streaming services such as Spotify, although revenue allocation has been criticised here for being unfairly small – this can be traced to the very large amounts demanded by record companies for licensing product whilst not being obliged to pay artists for such usage. On the other end, new technologies have allowed high standards of recording to be affordable to artists, removing dependency on large record companies to finance recordings, and keeping ownership in the hands of artists and smaller labels.

5. What would be the effects of the imbalance in the access and right use of technology in the music industry?

What imbalance are you talking about?

6. What are the main reasons for people that avoid the modern technology in the music industry?

There is some research that indicates a loss of some aspects of musical experience with digital recordings and some artists believe that analog recording technologies sound better based on their subjective experience. Most artists accept that there is little that can be done at the moment if they wish to have their music heard beyond a very small and local circle – there is always the hope that future technologies will improve the situation.

7. How do you think that disadvantaged persons could use technology for accessing the music?

This depends on what you mean by "disadvantaged". Physically disadvantaged people can have greater access to music through the internet and other computer-based technologies. Culturally or economically disadvantaged people may live in societies where these technologies are not available or not affordable.

ASHBURN MILLER

1. How would you describe the term technology?

For me, technology is just a cooler word for new ideas. Not much different than records, it's all just ideas in your head until you can put together a team to make your idea or technology a reality. Some technology propels us forward and some seem to send us backwards also like records ha,ha.

2. How do you react when dealing with a new technology?

Depends, 90% of the time I want to learn everything I can about some new technology and ill YouTube, everything I can about how to use it, but then there is times, like the past month in my life where I will just shut off that part of my mind. It can get so cluttered with all that stuff that I lose sight of the original mission, which is just to make music, which is older than any technology. Then I jump back into learning whatever I missed that month.

3. How would you consider the right use of technology?

I don't think there is an answer to that really. I mean we all hope technology isn't used for destructive purposes or to infringe on anyone's rights, but beyond that do with it what you will, or ignore. I know plenty of musicians that can sit with an acoustic guitar and captivate every part of you. Zero technology involved there just ears, heart, and brain. And some guys do the same thing using every new development there us in synth and computer software. I think you can get to the same place on any road. Sorry ling winded answer.

4. How technology affects the music industry?

How has it not. I mean mostly profits are nill. I just

don't see it as big as a negative as others in the business do. Music wasnt given to the universe to put people in mansions and nice cars. Not that those are bad things ha, ha we all want to better our lives, but It was supposed to stir the soul, and affect people. I think a lot of people lost sight of that and this is just the universe telling us that it's time to look at it differently. Get back to why we do it in the first place. Because it's exciting.

5. What would be the effects of the imbalance in the access and right use of technology in the music industry?

6. What are the main reasons for people that avoid the modern technology in the music industry?

I don't know that they do avoid it really, some maybe, maybe I don't understand the question?

7. How do you think that disadvantaged persons could use technology for accessing the music?

PAUL MAY

1. How would you describe the term technology?

It depends which hat I'm wearing at the time. As a producer; I would describe technology as a modern means and aid to achieving an end result, in either a quicker or a more precise fashion. But, as a guitarist / musician I would say it's a Godsend in most cases.

2. How do you react when dealing with a new technology?

It's a love hate thing for me! I really love what you can do with it, however, I hate all the re-learning process sometimes! But, I try to persevere because generally it's always worth the effort"

3. How would you consider the right use of technology?

That's quite a difficult one to nail down as so many different types of music nowadays wouldn't even exist without modern technology, particularly in the dance and clubbing scene'. I think the right use of technology would be to achieve an end result that couldn't be achieved any better naturally or to enhance any project further than is expected.

4. How technology affects the music industry?

Again, a bitter sweet combo, in as much that the world now has access to millions of artists worldwide via the net and iTunes, however the downside is that no sooner you have your album out via a record company a hundred pirate sites are giving it away free!

If you're a big enough act you can soak up the loss, but a little band that's trying to make a career this way is in trouble from the word go! But, the exposure can be amazing! On the plus side of things, the equipment and ideas that have now evolved for musicians and producers have made being able to create music quicker and easier than ever before. And the results you can achieve today compared to a decade ago is just frightening!

5. What would be the effects of the imbalance in the access and right use of technology in the music industry?

Probably the loss of originality and the loss of identity' due to the overuse of unnecessary technical tactics.

6. What are the main reasons for people that avoid the modern Technology in the music industry?

I think maybe 'old school' music industry, find it quite daunting to get to grips with after a lifetime of turning volume knobs on an amplifier and pushing manual faders on a mixer and then having to learn how to automate and program, which is understandable. But also, I think some of the artists and bands have understood   that   people   prefer   'songs'   and

'performance' more than, say the production, as a lot of indie bands have proved over the last decade. However, I love production myself, but I understand their concept. I also think some artists like to keep an authentic live take on their music, especially if they are good musicians and performers, so they would be minimalistic in their tech approach.

7. How do you think that disadvantaged persons could use technology for accessing the music?

I think technology can excel in this department on so many levels, it provides a way to make music at a half

decent level that can be heard by millions, if you're lucky, at the push of a button, with equipment that can produce a quality sound at next to nothing price! On that level, technology should be well received!

SUZI QUATRO

1. How would you describe the term technology?

WHATEVER IS AVAILABLE AT THE TIME IN THE HIGHEST QUALITY.. USUALLY SOMETHING YOU DON'T QUITE GET YET.

2. How do you react when dealing with a new technology?

CONFUSED.. I ONLY WANT TO LEARN, 'WHEN' I NEED TO LEARN IT AND NOT BEFORE

3. How would you consider the right use of technology?

DON'T OVER TAX YOURSELF.. KEEP IT WITHIN LIMITS.. NO SENSE GETTING A MIGRANE.

4. How technology affects the music industry?

TOO MUCH.. MUSIC WAS GREAT BECAUSE IT WAS REAL..TO PUT IT BLUNTLY.. HOW CAN IT BE CORRECT TO BE ABLE TO BEND SOMETIMES VOICE INTUNE.... THIS A NO NO.

5. What would be the effects of the imbalance in the access and right use of technology in the music industry?

TO LET MUSIC BREATH.. TO LET MUSIC LIVE.. TO LET MUSIC BE REAL.. PLAYED AND SUNG BY MUSICIANS AND SINGERS... FROM THE HEART.. NOT FROM THE MIXING DESK

6. What are the main reasons for people that

avoid the modern technology in the music industry?

THEY DON'T GET IT!!

7. How do you think that disadvantaged persons could use technology for accessing the music?

THE ONLY ADVANTAGE IS TO BE ABLE TO LISTEN TO STUFF ONLINE.. THAT'S IT!!!! MY HEART IS MY MUSIC.. I WISH MY MUSIC HAD THE SAME HEART.

MISS GUY

1. How would you describe the term technology?

Besides the obvious definition, I'd describe technology as a way of life or maybe even the way of life.

2. How do you react when dealing with a new technology?

I find new technology exciting and of course if I need help figuring something out, I don't hesitate to ask somebody.

3. How would you consider the right use of technology?

I think it should be used for personal enjoyment or as a tool for helping with everyday life. Unfortunately, people use it in ways that can be very dangerous.

4. How technology affects the music industry?

It's been helpful and many ways and detrimental in many ways that are obvious to most people. I didn't like it so much at first, but I've embraced it and actually love it.

5. What would be the effects of the imbalance in the access and right use of technology in the music industry?

I don't quite understand this question, sorry.

6. What are the main reasons for people that avoid the modern technology in the music industry?

I'm not sure really, I guess people like to do things the way they used to be done whether that's making music or buying music. Personally, I like the convenience technology offers for both making and buying music.

7. How do you think that disadvantaged persons could use technology for accessing the music?

Well, you can buy, or steal, music at the push of a button without leaving your house. I used to enjoy going shopping for records and CDs, but, I don't miss it now. I prefer getting music anytime of the day or night at the drop of a hat.

UDO HANTEN

© E.Patsialos I Synch 2009

1. How would you describe the term technology?

Technologie is a mixed blessing; on the one hand it

makes our life and work easier, on the other hand it destroys our cultures and values

2. How do you react when dealing with a new technology?

I take advantage of the fact that it saves me lifetime......

3. How would you consider the right use of technology?

There is no reasonable answer to this. Often things or technologies that are being celebrated today would prove wrong in the future

4. How technology affects the music industry?

To some extend it limits creativity and promotes banality and dilettantism. But then it also gives global access to unreachable works.

5. What would be the effects of the imbalance in the access and right use of technology in the music industry?

We can all see these effects; the music business has suffered a serious market break finally threatening the existence of many artists

6. What are the main reasons for people that avoid the modern technology in the music industry?

Maybe they do not have the knowledge, skills or abilities to use it. Another point could be a conservation of values and culture.

7. How do you think that disadvantaged persons could use technology for accessing the music?

Medicine has achieved considerable results not only giving access to technology but also as therapeutic action.

ANTHONY PHILLIPS

1. How would you describe the term technology?

I think that technology is everything to do with machines. Sometimes technology makes things less human. In the medicine world it is good because it saves people's lives.

2. How do you react when dealing with a new technology?

I am reacting in a very mixed way. I think that it is very beneficial to the musicians because they can create music without counting on a record company. Now through technology you can make your ideas real and the bands can be successful without having to do anything the record companies. The danger with the technology is that technology can reduce the natural creativity.

3. How would you consider the right use of technology?

Don't become a slave to it and don't become lazy. The danger when you use technology is that you may overanalyze and become too mechanistic. I have seen the recording engineers that are editing music without listening to it but just looking to it! This is quite scary. I think that the creativity should be the mother of technology and not technology leading the creativity.

4. How technology affects the music industry?

I think that makes things much more possible and I think that is fantastic. I also think that dance music becomes very similar and the songs have the same beat over time. The things become mechanistically.

5. What would be the effects of the imbalance in the access and right use of technology in the music industry?

I think that when technology leads the music, then the music has the danger of having a short life because not so many human beings are involved.

6. What are the main reasons for people that avoid the modern technology in the music industry?

Those people, particularly involved in the acoustic music, do not want to fall into the trap of having their music dominated by technology. The orchestrations in albums from bands like Beatles or Beach Boys were created by brain and not technology. I think that a lot of acoustic based musicians would use technology only when it helps them.

7. How do you think that disadvantaged persons could use technology for accessing the music?

I think that this is a perfect example of why technology is brilliant. Obviously technology would allow a disable person to be able of accessing and creating things. I think that the most powerful use of technology is to allow people that could not create in the recording studio, now to make them get these ideas down through the avenue of technology.

Another example is that people who cannot orchestrate, cannot write down music on a piece of paper, they can translate their orchestral score into reality. That can give people a lot of control and a lot of power and it is very positive.

COLIN BASS

1. How would you describe technology?

Technology is always in a state of flux. When I talk as a musician, then technology means to have a whole recording studio with a computer. The computer has a facility to do things that years ago you would have to pay a lot of money to hire a recording studio. This is a major change. The biggest change that affects the music business is the fact that musicians can record at home as I do, but also affects the way that people consume music. So we have the situation nowadays where the record company is an outdated concept. Record companies are still trying to find ways about controlling the business, but technology makes it impossible because people take what they want without having to pay or paying very little for it. It is a very complex subject because as we speak it is changing the whole nature of what we used to think as the music business. People can have the music they want, but also can make their own music much more easily. At the same time the fact that people are not paying as much for music anymore means that musicians cannot live from music anymore. Also recording studios cannot live from music because it is all about the businesses that they get. Most recording studios I know are turning themselves towards soundtracks, television work and games.

2. How do you react when dealing with a new technology?

The upside of new technology is that enables musicians to make sounds and it is a good thing. The downside is that by using technology people are getting used to low quality because most people will listen to music nowadays on a set of headphones. The way that people listen to music is completely changed. I still occasionally buy CDs and listen to them, but mostly if I want to hear something I will just go on YouTube if I want to know what is new and what is going on. Other times I am sitting on my studio working on other people's music or working on my own music. So what I think about, how do I react to it is that actually for me is a wonderful thing because it means that I can have a recording studio in my house and also I can move to the country side. I am able to do that because these days when I am producing other people's records and I mix everything at home, I send the results through the internet to the record companies or to the clients. I do not even have to see them or to go anywhere. Certainly we live in the information age, there is too much of it around. You listen to a song you like and think that it is very nice and before you buy for yourself a copy of it, you feel that other songs are also very nice. This happens because there is much music around. This is how things are changing and I can only say that because I know how it was like twenty years ago and I have been a musician for over forty years. So when I was coming up and learning by training, the only way to make a record was to find a record company company contract, if you could get one, and that was enough.

3. How would you consider the right use of technology?

There are a lot of things that I do not know how to do. Should everybody know how doing everything? I do not think so. Perhaps musicians in some countries are not able to produce music due to the local infrastructure or the local economy. But, if you want to do something, then you have to find out how doing it.

4. What are the main reasons for people that avoid the modern technology in the music industry?

Technology changes the music consumption and changes what the musicians think about music. When I was younger, as a musician, I thought I have got to write forty minutes of songs so that I have enough songs to make an LP record. The record company also wanted a single so I had to write something 3 minutes long. Now the musicians make music for the medium, so the medium has changed the way that artists look into music. And because technology is the medium, they make music for the technology.

They do not avoid technology, but they choose a different way of technology, people using an older form of technology. When there was more money to invest in the music industry then you had high quality recordings made. These days the quality of the recording is going down and people are getting used to it. I would not say that people are avoiding technology, but they are avoiding the latest technology. They are somehow putting faith and consuming music through another technology. Maybe it is a bit updated, but it is still technology and changed the music that was made in the first place. It is a bit of nostalgia, but the old technology sounded better. Today everything is compressed. It is funny because there are musicians or technicians who would love to spend 10.000 pounds on a new microphone and 20.000 pounds on a compressor.

JAMES KOTTAK

1. How would you describe the term technology?

Enables the impossible

2. How do you react when dealing with a new technology?

I try my best to learn and accept that it is only going

to become more of a part of our lives...embrace it!

3. How would you consider the right use of technology?

ART, SCIENCE, RESEARCH, ETC... fortunately OR unfortunately it is a big aspect of our military defence.

4. How technology affects the music industry?

From the phonogram to present day, mass music distribution would never have happened with out technology.

Currently, many abuse the privilege of the internet by using technology to acquire music for free. This has killed the entire music industry that once relied on sales.

5. What would be the effects from the imbalance in the access and right use of technology in the music industry?

We are seeing it daily...loss of royalties to artists. Lack of funds to invest in new artists from the labels.

6. What are the main reasons for people that avoid the modern technology in the music industry?

They are simply living in the past...if the good old days were so good, why did they ever change?

7. How do you think that disadvantaged persons could use technology for accessing the music?

Maybe there will be a way for the deaf to hear? The sky is the limit for all.

MARK KOHLER

1. How would you describe the term technology?

To me technology is a doctrine of a special topic. This can be anything we are dealing with day by day things like food, medicine, media etc. etc.

2. How do you react when dealing with a new

technology?

I'm trying to understand the thoughts of the inventor behind this and if it will bring some benefits to my life when I'm using it.

3. How would you consider the right use of technology?

It is important to understand all consequences of using it, what does it do to me and what does it do the society. Will it change the future in a positive direction and can everyone participate.

4. How technology affects the music industry?

Certain things seem to get uncontrollable, piracy in the music business is one of the issues. The access of affordable recording technology to basically everyone in the western civilisation will decrease the quality standard of creative music in terms of its commercial use on one side and on the other hand it will give creative people which could not afford a professional recording studio a chance to get their compositions released.

5. What would be the effects from the imbalance in the access and right use of technology in the music industry?

As mentioned before loss of quality.

6. What are the main reasons for people that

avoid the modern technology in the music industry?

Age, quality, fear of not understanding the abstract way of how something is working for example electronic storage of music on a chip instead of a magnetic tape.

7. How do you think that disadvantaged persons could use technology for accessing the music?

One example is the Evolution of hearing aids, or of medical surgery.

TOM BRUMPTON

1. How would you describe the term technology?

It's an incredibly broad term. Washing machines are a product of technology. Televisions, cars, mobile phones, even the wheel is a form of primitive technology. If I had to describe technology I suppose I'd go with progression. The progression of mankind through ideas and creation. Without technology, even the most basic forms of technology, we as a society couldn't function. If tomorrow morning a solar flare knocked out all telecommunications and fried circuitry across the globe, we'd still have basic equipment that constitutes as forms of technology that mankind both needs and could use to rebuild.

2. How do you react when dealing with a new technology?

I think I deal with new technology more inquisitively now than I did when I was younger. I'll play with a device a lot more; learn how it works, how to get the most out of it, get rid of programs and files that are kinda useless to me and stream line it.

3. How would you consider the right use of technology?

Using it in a manner that maximises the user's needs without infringing on the rights and well-being of others.

4. How technology affects the music industry?

In one way it's done great things. It allows bands across the world to spread the good word and allows people across the globe from all backgrounds to discover new artists. It's also helping the environment in that the invention of the MP3, the Kindle and the PDF has meant less plastic, paper and other raw materials are being used for these purposes.

However, on the flip side we've had Napster and other illegal sites like Pirate Bay and Limewire pop up and drain much needed funds out of the pockets of hard working artists. I've been thinking about this a lot recently and the more I think about it, the more I agree with Lars Ulrich and the actions he took over Napster. There's an entire culture of people that believe they're "entitled" to free music now for no good reason. Musicians deserve to earn from their art and this culture is putting a hold on young, up and coming bands doing just that.

So, as a promotional tool the internet is great. But as a market place the internet still has a Lot of holes that need plugging before companies, and more importantly independent artists of all crafts, can make a comfortable living through it.

5. What would be the effects from the imbalance in the access and right use of technology in the music industry?

We've been seeing the effects over the last couple of years. Record sales are at an all-time low, labels and bands are folding every day because they physically can't afford to continue, and people across the industry are having to re-think their business models in order to survive. It goes back to my argument of entitlement. Illegal downloading for this generation is, to some, on par with taping records from the radio by the generation beforehand. Frankly I don't see it that way, as at least with radio the artists got royalties and more often than not you'd keep the cheap, nasty tape copy with the swear words edited out until you could buy the records.

6. What are the main reasons for people that avoid the modern technology in the music industry?

I think it's simply a case of people being very set in their ways. For example I don't use Spotify. I've nothing against it, I just don't feel the need for it. I've got my records and if I'm curious about a band I'll check them out on either YouTube or iTunes. Technology will always progress, it's what it does. But people after a while just get comfortable with what they know and don't feel the need to change, and technology is no exception to that rule.

7. How do you think that disadvantaged persons could use technology for accessing the music?

People who don't have much money or maybe don't have direct access to records, for whatever reason, can check out new artists through sites like Spotify, YouTube, Last FM or Soundcloud. Reasons like this are definite bonuses for artists and fans alike, but I think the big issue is that a lot of people abuse the free flow of information and its lead on from there to the mass abundance of downloading and all the problems it's caused.

The internet is a double-edged sword; it can help break artists who would've never had a chance otherwise and it can help in reducing a massive record label to its knees. With that in mind, I genuinely hope one day artists and labels find a way to monetize things in a way that benefits everyone. I don't want to rip off our fans, not in the slightest. But the idea of people stealing music because someone told them it was OK, while bands foot massive bills for everything from production to gear isn't right and it's a massive problem that needs to be resolved.

STEVE HACKETT

1. How would you describe the term technology?

The flint was to the Stone Age man what the computer is to us today. It is the latest invention. Techniques and knowledge have their limitations. There are limits to human communication. There is always more to discover.

2. How do you react when dealing with a new technology?

I find it exciting.

3. How would you consider the right use of technology?

Machines have a special place but the human being is a technological marvel and we shouldn't need to exist in an entirely samplistic medium.

4. How technology affects the music industry?

It aids it enabling individuals to create their own channels, shop windows and styles.

5. What would be the effects from the imbalance in the access and right use of technology in the music industry?

Most of us would be out of a job if the robot Elvis manages to sing, dance and become the hero of your dreams.

6. What are the main reasons for people that avoid the modern technology in the music industry?

Vintage gear and vintage thinking often lend the creator a certain authenticity based on a traditional approach. The classical violinist considers owning a Stradivarius a passport to excellence.

7. How do you think that disadvantaged persons could use technology for accessing the music?

I've seen it happen with someone who has completely lost the motor functions with his body create a song and sing it wonderfully. He did this via a computer.

Conclusions And Recommendations

Digital divide is a factor that contributes negatively to the economic growth of the entertainment by denying nations and people access to technology and associated efficiencies in its use. Most emerging economies are unable to fully embrace the internet revolution due to various issues such as unfavourable economy, culture, location, education and politics. The resulting imbalance in technology's use between countries threatens the good relationships between them because feelings of insecurity and jealousy. The increasing use of mobile computing in the music industry offers hope to bridge the digital divide and reduces the associated problems. The attractive features of mobile computing include their small size, low cheap, ease of use and familiarity to most people.

Information and communication technology is going to play a very important role in the near future with the help of mobile computing as the concept for communication and information exchange among nations becomes a reality. We live in an information society and everything changes so quickly around us; so we do not want to loose the flow of information while the human movement is implemented. Information exchange with mobile computing should lead society to higher levels of progress. The introduction of mobile computing in the less developed countries and human minorities should have a strong impact in society's union and the humanistic mission for a democratic share of knowledge and better quality of life.

Recommendation of the semantic web

More research needs to be carried out in information technology, for instance Web 3.0 or semantic web which currently has more conceptual than implementation existence (Feigenbaum , 2007). Semantic Web is helping in the search engines by integrating information from various sources so that they are collectively useful (Liyang, 2007; Serewicz, 2010). It is the web of data with meaning in the sense that a computer program can learn enough about what the data means to process it (Berners, 1999). Semantic web thinks efficiently and by combining different sources of information, it displays more meaningful results during the search in web engines. The structure of the semantic web uses ontologies that are called explicit layers (Gruber, 2009). These anthologies help in the division of the web in a meaningful way by taking notice of plenty of parameters in the behavior of the internet user.

Digital divide refers to the lack of efficient use of technology as well. So during the search for keywords in search engines, the non-efficient search shows a sign of digital divide. For example when somebody is searching in Google for a music web store and makes spelling errors, writes unknown keywords or tries to write in the wrong text fields, then his behavior shows a non-efficient use of technology. When semantic web is in the process of learning from the user's behavior it has to be kept in mind that digital divide should be included in this intelligence and then display easier ways to search in Google for people with lack of skills. Semantic web could be a powerful tool in ICT1 and will help the less progressed governments to improve the competitiveness of the local human resources by using the web technology more efficiently.

Recommendation of the mobile phones

As the cost of buying a computer and the complex education required using it expand the digital divide (Servon, 2002), individuals are prevented from getting into internet technology which is crucial to the music industry. So there is a need for a device that would minimize these issues.

The devices that seem to have more opportunities to close the digital gap are the new mobile phones which have internet access and you can do almost everything that you have been previously doing with the use of a

---

[1] ICT stands for Information Communication Technology

home computer (Rainer and Cegielski, 2009). Nowadays mobile phones are being used not only for voice communication but they extend the word communication by exploring all the types of communication (video, text, file sharing, etc.) that your personal computer is implementing.

If digital divide is preventing the music market to grow efficiently and the local economies to benefit from this progression, then the technology's portability through the usage of mobile phones is very close to solving the problem. Mobile phones are already familiar to people with lower income because they are cheap enough to use for their daily communication, cheaper than a home computer (Banks, 2008). The fact that people are familiar with mobile phones makes them more ready to accept the change in technology and brave enough to experiment with it. Moreover, the small portable device is like a toy for them so it also adds an element of entertainment to their everyday life.

In the past there were fights among the social classes regarding the imbalance in the share of wealth and education between the poor and the rich people. Now today's governments are called to solve the problem of injustice in the share of technology between the nations. This is something that is already in progress with the International Finance Corporation who has spent millions of US dollars in small countries such as the Democratic Republic of Congo, Madagascar, Malawi, Sierra Leone and Uganda. The goal of this funding was the maintaining and upgrading of the existing mobile networks in a way that the smaller countries can keep in touch with the communication structure in the developed nations (Banks, 2008).

Recommendation of the ABC technique

The current academic research is trying to find out what prevents disadvantaged populations from adopting the changes of the digital music industry and why the digital divide effect is being increased. While John Fisher's theory model is a suitable model for a survey there is an interesting theory that can help in finding the solution to the problem. The ABC technique (Tschudi, 1977) was introduced by Finn Tschudi in order to show why people do not want to change or what prevents them from changing.

Tschudi's theory is based on examining the current status in comparison with the desired status and mentioning the advantages and disadvantages in both situations. The steps of the process are the following:

- Identifying which is the current and which is the desired situation.
- Referring to all the disadvantages in the current situation and the advantages by moving to the desired situation.

- Identifying all the disadvantages of moving to the new situation.
- Comparing the advantages and disadvantages of moving to a new situation or remaining in the old situation.

Analyzing the values / weightings, additionally a start of discussion between the researcher and the respondent. The scope of the discussion is to find out how the respondent will overcome the barriers of moving to the new situation.

In order to understand better the implication of this theory, I use the example of the smoking habit (Fisher, 2011):

A	Current state	Desired state
	I smoke 40 a day	I want to stop smoking
B	Disadvantages	Advantages
	× Expensive	× Have more money
	× Bad for your health	× Less chance of lung cancer, etc.
	× Smokers cough	× Taste food
	× Bad breath	
	× Food tasteless	
	× Clothes/hair smell of smoke	
	× Antisocial now	
C	Advantages	Disadvantages

		Table: The ABC technique
× De-stresses me	× Put on weight	
× Lets me take a break (and if I leave a tricky job for a smoke I usually find I've cracked it when I get back)	× Stuck at desk all day	
	× Miss friends	
	× Get irritable	
	× Get stressed up	
	× Enjoy the taste	
× Social (in the smoking shelter chat, get latest gossip, meet mates, etc.)	× Withdrawal symptoms	The A row is the identification of the current state where someone is smokin
	× Always smoked	
	× I actually don't want too!	
× Something to do with my hands	And anyway the chances of me getting cancer, etc. are pretty slim - my dad smoked all his life and he's as fit as a fiddle!	

g and the desired state where the same person wants to stop smoking. Row B shows the disadvantages of the current situation and the advantages of moving to the new situation. Row C shows which are the advantages and disadvantages from not moving to the new situation. During the analysis of the rows, if row C includes more important things than row B then the respondent will deny in moving to the new situation. Of course ABC technique can be combined with John Fisher's transition curve in order to find out how disadvantaged populations that are afraid of buying music through the internet can move forward which is the last stage of John Fisher's emotional stages. This is a technique that requires personal interviews with the respondents because the process is interactive and a survey cannot be used to solve the problem. So if the ABC technique will be applied to the Transition Curve theory then the new table would look like this:

A	Current state	Desired state
	I am afraid of buying music on the internet	I want to move forward on buying music on the internet
B	Disadvantages	Advantages
	- Damages of the physical products of music through the time - Being out of fashion - Hard to find physical products of music after a few years	- Save time - Being modern - Being innovative
C	Advantages	Disadvantages
	- Save money - Being oldschool is cool - Social (people of my age still buying	- Wasting time in learning the new technology - Get stressed up - I actually don't

	vinyl)	want too!

Table: ABC technique meets transition curve theory

Of course the values that are mentioned in table 27 are just an example of how the combination between the 2 models would look like. Further research is needed for the exact definition of the new model and correct advantages and disadvantages of each situation.

Recommendation of the mobile social networking

If fear is the feeling that prevents the disadvantaged populations from accepting the change in the music technology and their life, then this social group needs a way so as to trust technology. Social trust through the exchange of information will be the solution to the problem. Social trust is a phenomenon that will be implemented by the extensive use of the social networking.

The role of exporting information (and especially the way that information is treated) is very important in the current society. We live in an information society where information is considered the ultimate value for economic growth of humanity and a significant tool to build the future for the next generations (Infosoc, 2010). Information is therefore the key for raising the cultural capital. The movement of people within the hierarchy of the social classes is called social mobility (Devine, 1997) and the equal access to information is considered to be one of the pre-requirements for social mobility (Alonso and Oiarzabal, 2010).

If we consider the foregoing discussion with the most popular triggers of social mobility then we find the social capital that is produced through virtual communities and social networking. One of the latest trends in virtual communities is the mobile social networking where groups of people with common interests are connected with the use of a mobile phone (Butler, 2006).

The extended Wi-Fi networks at various locations and the progressive technologies of mobile phones transfer the social networking action from the static computers to mobile computing. This trend affects the important social networking sites like Facebook, Twitter, and Go Mobile; and raises the popularity of social networking to mobile phone users who may not have had the opportunity to experience social networking before due to not owning a personal computer (Rutledge, 2008). The trend of mobile social networking is very popular in Europe and the Pacific Rim where the use of personal computers is less than the USA (Gillin, 2009). In the UK almost a quarter of all the smart phone users use mobile devices for accessing social networking (Ofcom, 2010). In general, portable devices are small, cheap and popular because they always come up with new software updates. The small size of the screen could be a disadvantage but there are always alternate solutions with screen projectors in large surfaces of the home, or in the office. Today there are enterprises that encourage the use of mobile social networking in the office so as to boost employee morale, create innovative ideas and unite employees under the company's internal network (Gillin, 2009). The mobile social networking within companies helps the global distribution of the work expertise and enhances the power of team working.

There are two types of mobile social networks regarding the access in the network. The first has collaboration with Wi-Fi companies who support these virtual communities by distributing to members the default web pages of the communities. The second category of mobile social networks operates on their own without any special promotion through other communication carriers.

The mobile virtual communities that are created have been very popular due to the increased rate of information sharing and social trust that is developed among users (Falcone, Barber and Singh, 2008). The knowledge that comes out of the community's interaction is valuable because it is a product of a democratic process where everyone has the right to express his own point of view. There are usually one or more moderators of the forum that monitor discussions and make sure that there is no abuse of the community by users and that the operation of the community meets the initial mission. Each virtual community often has a unique mission and the outcome of the community usually depends on the creator. The majority of mobile virtual communities have a non-profit mission which could be medical help, art, society contribution, travel experience, philosophy, sports, technology and popularity and more. Other communities naturally also exist with profitability mission regarding business intelligence, marketing and sales and other. Moreover, the mobility encourages people to reply instantly to information. Thus, the speed of interaction increases the rate of the distributed knowledge and the received information is updated because people transmit knowledge the time it is created.

One of the most important outcomes of mobile virtual communities is social capital which triggers social mobility (Dasgupta, 2006). The social capital is a result of information exchanging between the users and the constant interaction between the members of the community based on trust. A study by the Society for the New Communication Research showed that people agree with the statement that "they choose products based on other customer's experiences which were shared online (Gillin, 2009). Another research conducted by Nielsen showed that consumers referred to other customers about being their trusted source of information (Nielsen, 2009). There are mobile social networks that operate as an intelligent search engine and combine results from other virtual communities to offer the smartest reply for people's questions.

The mobile virtual communities unite people with differences in race, age, and economic status under the umbrella of the need for information and understanding; so, it builds trust between the members of the community. Such understanding and familiarity with each other sometimes result in physical meetings which inevitably often enhance the trust relationship.

Social mobility fits perfectly with human mobility because they share a common ground in movement and there is always the need for information exchange. Mobile computing is playing the role of the intermediary between the two types of mobility, with the creation of mobile communities that preserve the ethics and democracy of the community culture. The character of virtual communities in mobile social networking creates two of the requirements that society needs to lead people in the upward movement within human society: trust and e-democracy. Social trust occurs because the mission of the forum is to share the power of knowledge by helping each other in a democratic way. The conclusion here is that the social trust of mobile virtual communities leads to social capital which enhances social mobility.

The efficient use of ICT must include the improvement of the existing wireless networks by offering more free spots for mobile computing users and more bandwidth for exchanging of information. The progress in filling the gap of the digital divide should have multiple effects on the economy and society. The solving of imbalance in the distribution and technology's usage among people should lead us to become a more democratic community where everyone, as imagined by proponents as Khosrowpour (2003), will have equal rights to access to technology and equal rights for access to society's process such as elections and education.

The access to technology for all should offer new opportunity for scientists to rise from emerging countries and contribute to new technologies within the information society, so that they could raise the production industry. Moreover, the country of the scientist's origination may have a competitive advantage of the human capital and knowledge management that may be exported to other countries as well (Zaqqa, 2006).

Appendixes

These are some humorous examples of famous classic rock stars or their publicists, who refused to answer the interview questions. The persons shall remain nameless for obvious reasons.

Re: ⬛⬛⬛⬛⬛ interview request

To Billy Yfantis

Billy,
I'm gonna pass
The subject matter is not of that much interest to me
as a 70 year old. I now mostly think oy myself as retired,

Re: Interview request for a book (Inquiry #335229)

From: ⬛⬛⬛⬛⬛⬛⬛⬛⬛⬛⬛⬛⬛⬛
To: Byfantis@yahoo.com
Sent: Wednesday, September 25, 2013 4:59 PM
Subject: Re: Interview request for a book (Inquiry #335229)

"Thank you for your inquiry. Although ⬛⬛⬛⬛ & ⬛⬛⬛⬛ still play a few select dates each year in order to benefit John's family foundation, he is effectively out of the "music business" and no longer participates in promo activities, etc."

Photo Credits

Steve Hackett image: Lesley Wood
Eric Norlander image: Eric Nielsen
Miss Guy image: Veronica Ibarra
Udo Hanten: E. Patsialos

References and further sources

Alonso, A. and Oiarzabal, P. (2010) Diasporas in the New Media Age: Identity, Politics, and Community. Reno: University of Nevada Press.

Amjad, U. (2004) Mobile Computing and Wireless Communications. Michigan: NGE Solutions, Inc.

Banks, K. (2008) Mobile Phones and the Digital Divide [Online] Available: http://www.pcworld.com/article/149075/mobile_phones _and_the_digital_divide.html [28 Nov 2010].

Bell, D. (1999) The coming of post industrial society. New York: Basic Books.

Bernardo, M. and Bogliolo, A. (2005) Formal methods for mobile computing: 5th International School on Formal Methods for the Design of Computer, Communication, and Software Systems, SFM-Moby 2005, Bertinoro, Italy, April 26-30, 2005 : advanced lectures. Urbino: Springer.

Berners, L. (1999) Semantic Web definition [Online] Available: http://www.w3.org [28 Nov 2010].

Besser, H. (2011) The next digital divides [Online] Available: http://www.tcla.gseis.ucla.edu/divide/politics/besser.html [16 Feb 2011].

Businessballs (2011) Process of personal change [Online] Available:

http://www.businessballs.com/personalchangeprocess.ht m [13 Mar 2011].

Butler, P. (2006) Well connected: releasing power and restoring hope through kingdom partnerships Colorado Springs: Biblica.

Caribbean 360 Disabled People A Growing Tourism Market [Online] Available: http://www.caribbean360.com/index.php/travel/25982.h tml [18 Feb 2011].

Chadwick, A. (2009) Routledge handbook of Internet politics New York: Taylor & Francis.

Chen, Z. (2007) Antennas for portable devices. West Sussex: John Wiley and Sons.

Christman, E. (2010) Digital Divide. Billboard.biz [Online] Available: http://www.billboard.biz/bbbiz/content_display/magazin e/upfront/e3i12fe2557a9382597671a522cc1cc901d# [18 Feb 2010].

Clark-Meads, J. (1999) Bulgaria stamps out CD piracy. Billboard magazine, 22 May 1999, p. 48.

Council of Europe (2009), Parliamentary Assembly Working Papers - 2008 Ordinary Session, Fourth Part, 29 September-3-october 2008 - 2009, Volume 7.

Dasgupta, S. (2006) Encyclopedia of virtual communities and technologies London: Idea Group Inc (IGI).

Delanty, G. (2010) Community New York: Taylor &

Francis.

Devine, F. (1997) Social class in America and Britain, Edinburgh: Edinburgh University Press.

Dutton, W. (2005) Transforming enterprise: the economic and social implications of information technology Massachusetts: MIT Press.

Dynamic Europe (2010) Dynamic Controls Software [Online] Available: http://www.dynamiccontrols.com [8 Apr 2011].

ESCWA (2002) Summary of the Annual Review of Developments in Globalization and Regional Integration in the Countries of the ESCWA Region by the United Nations Economic and Social Commission for Western Asia New York: United Nations.

Falcone, R., Barber, S. and Singh, M. (2008) Trust in Agent Societies 11th International Workshop, TRUST 2008, Estoril, Portugal, May 12 -13, 2008. Revised Selected and Invited Papers New York: Springer.

Feigenbaum, L. (2007) The Semantic Web in Action. Scientific American, pp 90-97, December 2007.

Fisher, J. (2011) The ABC technique [Online] Available: http://www.c2d.co.uk/page14.htm [20 May 2011].

Gillespie, T. (2007) Wired shut: copyright and the shape of digital culture. Massachusetts: MIT Press.

Gillin, P. (2009) Mobile Social Networking: The New Ecosystem [Online] Available:

http://www.virtualizationadmin.com/ [28 Nov 2010].

Gruber, T. (2009) Ontology Encyclopedia of Database Systems [Online] Available: http://tomgruber.org/writing/ontology-definition-2007.htm [28 Nov 2010].

Heylin, C. (2003) Bootleg: the rise & fall of the secret recording industry London: Omnibus Press.

Infosoc (2010) Information Society [Online] Available: http://www.infosoc.gr/infosoc/en-UK/default.htm [28 Nov 2010].

Jesperson, K. (2010) iPad May Make Communication Possible for Disabled People [Online] Available: http://www.suite101.com/content/ipad-may-make-communication-possible-for-disabled-people-a227516 [13 Apr 2011].

Khosrowpour, M. (2003) Information technology and organizations: trends, issues, challenges & solutions, Volume 1, London: Idea Group Inc (IGI).

Kim, W. (2001) The human society and the Internet: Internet-related socio-economic issues Proceedings of the First International Conference Human Society @Internet 2001, Seoul, Korea, July 4-6, 2001. New York: Springer.

Langan, M. (1998) Welfare: needs, rights, and risks New York: Routledge.

Langer, A. (2002) Applied ecommerce: analysis and engineering for ecommerce systems. West Sussex: Wiley.

Lazarus, W. and Mora, F. (2000) Online Content for Low-Income and Underserved Americans: The Digital Divide's New Frontier. Santa Monica: Children's Partnership.

Lee, Y., Ho Kang, B. and Slezak D. (2010) Future Generation Information Technology", Proceedings of the Second International Conference, FGIT 2010, Jeju Island, Korea, December 13-15, 2010. Heidelberg: Springer

Li, Q., Stankovic J., Hanson M., Barth A. and Lach J. (2009) Accurate, Fast Fall Detection Using Gyroscopes and Accelerometer-Derived Posture Information", International Conference on Body Sensor Networks, Berkeley: University of California.

Lister, K. (2011) IODA Africa Launches To Bring Local, Sub-Saharan African Music To Fans Throughout The Continent And Around The World. cited in Reuters [Online] Available: http://www.reuters.com/article/2011/01/23/idUS18148 +23-Jan-2011+MW20110123 [19 March 2011].

Livi, E. (2008) Information Technology and New Business Models in the Tourism Industry, 8th Global Conference on Business and Economics, Florence, Italy, October 18-19.

Liyang, Y. (2007) Introduction To Semantic Web And Semantic Web Services New York: Chapman and Hall / CRC.

Mayrer, S. E. (2003) What is a disadvantaged group?, Minneapolis: Effective Communities Project.

Michael A. and Salter, B. (2006) Mobile marketing: achieving competitive advantage through wireless technology. Oxford: Butterworth-Heinemann.

Monroe, B. J. (2004) Crossing the digital divide: race, writing, and technology in the classroom New York: Columbia University.

Moore, F. (2011) Digital Music Report 2011 [Online] Available: http://www.ifpi.org/content/library/DMR2011.pdf [13 Apr 2011].

Nielsen Research Group For Social Networking, Women use Mobile more than Men [Online] Available: http://blog.nielsen.com/nielsenwire/online_mobile/for-social-networking-women-use-mobile-more-than-men [20 Dec 2010].

Norris, P. (2001) Digital divide: civic engagement, information poverty, and the Internet worldwide Cambridge: Cambridge University Press.

NTIA (2002) A nation online. How Americans are expanding their use of the internet. Washington D.C.: NTIA, US Department of Commerce, Economics and Statistic Administration.

Ofcom, (2010) Consumers spend almost half of their waking hours using media and communications [Online] Available: http://media.ofcom.org.uk/2010/08/19/consumers-spend-almost-half-of-their-waking-hours-using-media-and-communications [20 Dec 2010].

Online Africa (2009) Why Africa won't need iTunes [Online] Available: http://www.oafrica.com/broadband/itunes/# [28 Nov 2010].

Quinones, S., Kirshshtein, R. and Loy, N. (1998) Educator's Guide to Evaluating the Use of Technology in School & Classrooms US Department of Education

Rainer, R. and Cegielski, C. (2009) Introduction to Information Systems: Enabling and Transforming Business West Sussex: John Wiley and Sons.

Rakowski, N. (2011) Maslow's Hierarchy of Needs Model - the Difference of the Chinese and the Western Pyramid on the Example of Purchasing Luxurious Products Norderstedt: GRIN Verlag.

Reworking Maslow's Pyramid (2010). New York Times, 16 July.

Reza, F. (2005) Mobile computing principles: designing and developing mobile applications with UML and XML. Cambridge: Cambridge University Press.

Ruckert, M. (2005) Understanding MP3: syntax, semantics, mathematics, and algorithms. Berlin: Spring Science.

Rutledge, P. (2008) The Truth about Profiting from Social Networking New Jersey: FT Press.

Sallis, E. and Jones G. (2002) Knowledge management in education: enhancing learning & education London: Routledge.

Schiller, J. (2003) Mobile communications. Essex: Pearson Education.

Serewicz, W. (2010) Do we need bigger buckets or better search engines?: The challenge of unlimited storage and semantic web search for records management Records Management Journal, Vol. 20, Issue 2, pp 172-181.

Servon, L. (2002) Bridging the digital divide: technology, community, and public policy Oxford: Wiley-Blackwell.

Stone In Science, H. (2010) 4 Context-Aware Computing Technologies from Intel That Will Shape the Future [Online] Available: http://www.chipchick.com/2010/10/context-aware-computing.html [20 Dec 2010].

Tschudi, F. (1977) Loaded and Honest Questions, in Bannister D (ed), New Perspectives in Personal Construct Theory. London: Academic Press.

Turmusani, M. (2003) Disabled people and economic needs in the developing world: a political perspective from Jordan Hampshire: Ashgate Publishing, Ltd.

Tregaskis, C. (2004) Constructions of disability: researching the interface between disabled and non-disabled people. New York: Routledge.

Wood, A. , Stankovic, J., Virone, G., Selavo, L., He, Z., Cao, Q., Doan, T., Wu, Y., Fang, L. and Stoleru R. (2008) Context-Aware Wireless Sensor Networks for Assisted-Living and Residential Monitoring Department of Computer Science, University of Virginia.

Xiaoming, H. and Chow, S. K. (2004) Factors affecting Internet development: An Asian survey [Online] Available: http://firstmonday.org/issues/issue9_2/hao/ [28 Nov 2010].

ABOUT THE AUTHOR

Billy Yfantis holds an MSc in Information Technology (University Of The West Of Scotland) and an MSc in Information Security (Luleå University of Technology), moreover he is the author of scientific articles published worldwide. Technology as a medium and music as a mission led him to experiment with unorthodox sounds and machines since the late 1990s.

Bibliography

V. Yfantis, "The Commercial Exploitation Of Color As A Consumer Stimulus" (Greek Edition), Createspace, 2013.

V. Yfantis, "The Lost Lyrics" (Greek Edition), Createspace, 2013.

V. Yfantis, "Punk Goes Science: The Academic Punk Bibliography",CreateSpace, 2014

V. Yfantis, "City Streets Of Europe", Lulu, 2017

Contact: Byfantis@yahoo.com
Website: www.skylight.gr